WILDLY WEIRD
BUT TOTALLY TRUE
AUSTRALIA

Australian Fun Facts, True Stories and Trivia

A Hello Sydney Kids book, created on the lands of the Wiradjuri people, Australia.

Copyright © 2022 Seana Smith
ISBN 978-0-6456637-0-9

All rights reserved.

No portion of this book may be reproduced in any form without written permission from the publisher or author, except as permitted by U.S. copyright law.

This publication is designed to provide accurate and authoritative information in regard to the subject matter covered. It is sold with the understanding that neither the author nor the publisher is engaged in rendering legal, investment, accounting or other professional services. While the publisher and author have used their best efforts in preparing this book, they make no representations or warranties with respect to the accuracy or completeness of the contents of this book and specifically disclaim any implied warranties of merchantability or fitness for a particular purpose. No warranty may be created or extended by sales representatives or written sales materials. The advice and strategies contained herein may not be suitable for your situation. You should consult with a professional when appropriate. Neither the publisher nor the author shall be liable for any loss of profit or any other commercial damages, including but not limited to special, incidental, consequential, personal, or other damages.

Book Cover & Illustrations by Joy Lora

1st edition 2022

Table of Contents

Honestly! Amazing True Facts	1
World Records + World Firsts	9
Funny Place Names	14
Geographic Joys	27
Incredible Indigenous Australia	40
Astounding Animals	44
Wacky History + Politics	64
Phenomenal Places	67
Strange Sweet Stuff	75
Freaky Farming + Food Facts	79
Crazy Culture	82
Tough Trees	85
Sydney Opera House Oddities	87
Stunning Cities	89
Final Five Fun Facts	92
Thank You!	94
Author Biography	95

Honestly! Amazing True Facts About Australia

Wombat poo is square.

Why is a wombat poo square in shape? Seriously, wombats poo up to one hundred cube-shaped poos every night.

The wombat is the only animal to poo in a square to almost cube shape.

"I have never seen anything this weird in biology" said Georgia Institute of Technology's Patricia Yang who studies the intersection of fluid dynamics and biology.

Yang's groundbreaking wombat poo research used wombats that had been euthanised after being struck by cars. She found that in the final part of the wombat's long digestive tract there was variety in the elasticity of the intestinal wall and this created the separated cube shapes of the wombat poo during digestion and contraction. In other mammals the contractions of the muscles of the intestines are consistent all around. Her 2021 article in the journal Soft Matter is titled 'Intestines of non-uniform stiffness mould the corners of wombat faeces'.

But why did the wombat evolve to have this six-sided poo?
Perhaps it is because they live in hilly areas and they need their poo not to roll off the rocks they poo on so that they could mark their territory efficiently.

But really, who knows?

Anyway, don't be fooled next time you see a square-looking chocolate-coloured 'treat' on a rock.

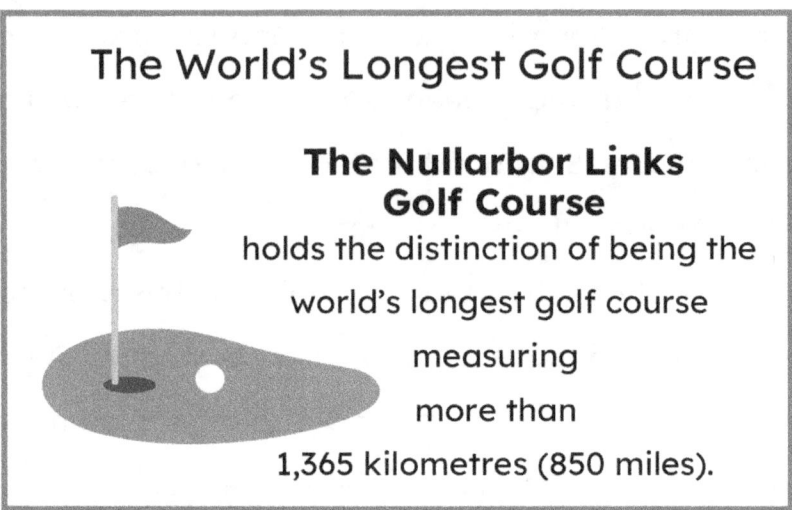

The World's Longest Golf Course

The Nullarbor Links Golf Course holds the distinction of being the world's longest golf course measuring more than 1,365 kilometres (850 miles).

The 18 holes are spread amongst the towns and roadhouses that are strung out across the Nullarbor Plain along the 1,664-kilometre (1,034-mile) Eyre Highway.

Completing each hole in the golf course makes this long drive more interesting and has encouraged visitors to spend more time in the little towns they pass through.

Australia is the world's smallest continent.

Australia at 7,692,024 km² is the sixth largest country in the world after

1) Russia   17,098,242 km²
2) Canada 9,879,750 km²
3) China   9,600,013 km²
4) USA   9,525,067 km²
5) Brazil   8,515,770 km²

Is Australia the largest island in the world?
The answer is NO.

Some people say that Australia is the largest island in the world. However, that is false. Australia can't be called an island because an island is a land mass that is surrounded entirely by water and is 'smaller than a continent'. Since Australia is a continent, it cannot be called an island.

So next time somebody says that Australia is the largest island in the world, remember to politely share this fact with them.

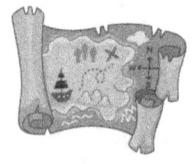 # Facts About the Name Australia

The name Australia came from an ancient map!
The name Australia was first seen on an ancient map created by the Greek cartographer, Claudius Ptolemy in 200AD. He believed that there must be a southern continent to balance the northern continents so he added it to his world map and called it Terra Australis Incognita, which means the unknown southern land.

Australia was also called New Holland
The first European explorer to reach the southern continent was the Dutch explorer Willem Janszoon on a voyage from Java in 1606. His countryman Abel Tasman sailed along the northern coastline in 1644 and named the land New Holland, a name that stuck.

From Terra Australis to Australia
The name Terra Australis was used in an 1804 map by English explorer and cartographer Matthew Flinders, as suggested by Sir Joseph Banks. It was Flinders who recommended that the name be converted to 'Australia' as it is more pleasing to the ear.

Formally adopting the name Australia

In 1817, Governor Lachlan Macquarie recommended that the name 'Australia' be formally adopted. In 1824, the British Admiralty agreed that the continent should be officially called Australia. So the name Australia simply means 'southern.'

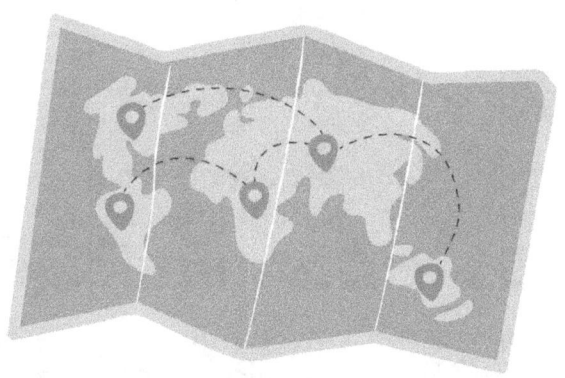

A cartographer is a person who draws maps and indicates the names of the land masses and oceans.

The World's Longest Highway

Highway 1

Australia boasts of having the longest highway in the world. Highway 1 is 14,500 kilometres (9,000 miles) long and is considered a giant 'ring road' because it follows the entire coastline of mainland Australia.

Melbourne was once called
Batmania

However, it's not because the colonists were fans of the caped crusader. John Batman was the founder of the early settlement on the Yarra River.

Batmania was officially renamed Melbourne on 10 April, 1837, by Governor Richard Bourke.

This was in honour of the then British Prime Minister, Lord Melbourne.

Is the Dingo Fence longer than the Great Wall of China?

The answer is NO.

The Dingo Fence is 5,614 kilometres (3,488 miles) long. Many people mistakenly believe it is longer than the Great Wall Of China. It is not! The Dingo Fence is about one-quarter of the total length of the various sections of the Great Wall. The Dingo Fence is, however, the longest fence in the world.

The Dingo Fence was built to keep marauding dingo and wild dogs out of the sheep grazing territory south of it. It worked! The sheep were safer and there were also big increases in the population of kangaroos.

The fence is 1.7 metres high.

It is, in fact, officially called the Dog Fence in South Australia and the Wild Dog Barrier Fence in Queensland.

World Records + World Firsts

Australians hold many world records.

Here are some of the weirdest:

World's Loudest Burp

Neville Sharp holds the world's record for the loudest burp with 112.4 decibels. That is louder than the sound of a drill which is around 90 decibels. He's less than 3 decibels shy of beating the trombone, the world's loudest instrument, with a recorded maximum sound of 115 decibels.

Most Underpants Worn At Once

Steve Jacobs broke his own record of 247 pairs by wearing 266 pairs of underpants on November 15, 2012. It looks simple, but really, it was exhausting as he had to keep his balance while withstanding the pressure from all 266 elastic waistbands. Not easy!

Fastest 100-metre Egg & Spoon Race

Do you enjoy running in an egg and spoon race? Could you beat 2008 Olympic champion hurdler Sally Pearson in the 100-metre egg and spoon race? Probably not!
Sally finished the race in 16.59 seconds so, by the time you read this paragraph, she would've already won.

World's Oldest Skydiver

In 2018, 102-year-old (and 193 days) Irene O'Shea became the world's oldest skydiver at Langhorne Creek in South Australia. She snatched the record from Kenneth Meyer of the US who was 21 days younger when he skydived. Her record-breaking jump was Irene's third skydive. She had celebrated turning 100 by skydiving and then returned a year later for her second jump.

World Record For Most Push-ups in 12 Hours

Is your dad or brother a fitness enthusiast? Tell them about this amazing record. In 2021, Jarrad Young from Queensland set the record for the most push-ups done in 12 hours, with 20,085. He also holds the record for the most clap push-ups done in one hour with, 3,054 push-ups.

World's Largest Number of Stargazers

The Australian Broadcasting Corporation hosted Stargazing Live in 2018, when over 40,000 people looked at the stars and moon simultaneously across many locations. This broke the previous world record which had also been held by Australia (7,960 people).

The low humidity, low air pollution and lack of population (and therefore lights) make the Australian outback one of the best places in the world for stargazing.

World's Most Successful Speedcuber

Feliks Zemdegs is an Australian Rubik's cube speedsolver. He is the only speedcuber ever to win the World Cube Association World Championship twice (in 2013 and 2015). He is considered the most successful speedcuber of all time with 121 world records, 210 continental records, and 6 national records.

World's Largest Dessert Pizza

The record for the world's largest dessert pizza is held by Crust Gourmet Pizza Bar. The pizza was created on 25 September, 2016, at the Gold Coast Convention Centre at Broadbeach. Its total surface area was 20.03 square metres (215.60 square feet). The pizza's length was 46.6 metres and width was 0.43 metres. Its toppings included fruit, meringue and cinnamon crumble.

Most Number Of Plates Smashed in 30 Seconds

 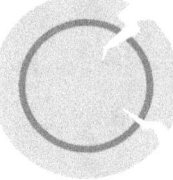

Smashing plates is traditionally used to signal the end and the beginning, to ward off evil spirits, and to express abundance. Con Damouras, a young immigrant from Greece set the record for the greatest number of plates smashed in 30 seconds on 17 April, 2005, in Sydney. He smashed 86 plates in 30 seconds and made all the Greek-Australians proud of him.

Longest Marbles Marathon

Do you still play marbles with other kids? Imagine playing it for 26 straight hours. That's what Michael and Jenna Grey did in 2006. They played marbles for non-stop 26 hours on 11-12 February, 2006 at First Fleet Park, The Rocks, Sydney, Australia.

Longest Plank in the World

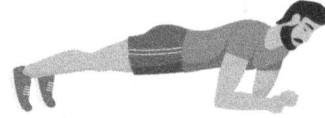

On 6 August, 2021, Daniel Scali beat the previous world's record for the longest plank (8 hours and 15 minutes) with his amazing plank record of 9 hours, 30 minutes & 1 second!

The World's First Seat Belt Law

Safety is a priority in Australia and in 1967 the state of South Australia was the first to mandate seatbelts in the front seats of cars. So be proud and always make sure to buckle up.

Funny Place Names

We all love animals and it's funny to see places named after them. In Australia, there are a lot of famous places and tourist spots that are named after animals found in that area. Some places were named after animals they resemble.

Elephant Rocks in West Australia are huge granite boulders that look like a herd of elephants.

Cow Bay
in the Daintree in Far North Queensland was named after dugongs.

Dugongs are called sea cows as they graze slowly on seagrass beds and they are as large as cows.

Heron Island can be found at the southern end of the Great Barrier Reef but, ironically, no herons live there..

The birds seen by Francis Blackwood as he sailed by on the HMS Fly in 1843 were actually eastern reef egrets.

However, egrets are a type of heron that's a little smaller & with darker legs, so he was almost correct.

Heron vs Egret

Taller
Bigger beaks
Orange legs

Plumes on head all year round

Smaller
Smaller beaks
Dark legs

Only have plumes during mating season

Hawks Nest

in New South Wales was named for the large hawk nest in a tree that was used as a navigational marker to indicate the entrance to Port Stephens.

Emu Bay

in South Australia is famous for its white sandy beaches while Emu Park in Queensland is a pretty seaside town with a famous Singing Ship Monument.

Black swans are native to Australia and there are several places named after them such as the **Swan Reach** in South Australia, Swan Hill in Victoria and Swan River in Perth.

Pelican at Lake Macquarie in New South Wales is named after the pelican, Australia's largest flying bird.

Eaglehawk Neck

is both a small town and a narrow isthmus between the Tasman and Forestier peninsulas.

The isthmus was known as The Neck and is only 100 metres wide at its narrowest.

When there was a penal colony at Port Arthur a Dog Line stretched across this isthmus: dogs were chained along a line to prevent escaped prisoners getting through. How scary!

Eaglehawk is another name for the wedge-tailed eagle which is common in that area of Tasmania.

Crows Nest in Queensland was not named after an actual crow. It was named after a local Indigenous man whom settlers named Jimmy Crow.

Jimmy helped the first colonist with information and advice and they called his camping spot Jimmy Crow's Nest.

A statue in the middle of the town honours him.

Salmon Beach is a fishing beach in Western Australia with wild surf that is generally not safe for swimming unless you are a salmon.

Shark Bay in West Australia does indeed have an abundance of sharks. It was William Dampier who named that area in 1699 after catching an 11-foot shark.

Fish Creek

in Gippsland, Victoria was named after the river blackfish that can be caught in the creek.

Lizard Island

is an island within a national park and is the northernmost island resort on the Great Barrier Reef. James Cook named the island in 1770 after its most common reptile, the yellow-spotted monitor lizard (Varanus panoptes).

Two places named after seals are Seal Bay and Seal Rocks.

Seal Bay
in South Australia is a conservation park that was formed to protect a colony of resident Australian sea lions.

Seal Rocks
in New South Wales were named after the Australian fur seals that were often seen on the rocks near the Sugarloaf Point Lighthouse.

Penguin in Tasmania is named after the little penguins (Eudyptula minor) that are native to the southern parts of Australia and Tasmania.

Some of the streets in the town of Penguin are penguin-themed and there is a large penguin statue.

Little penguins are different from the Adelie and emperor penguins seen in the movies Happy Feet and Madagascar. Little penguins weigh only one kilogram and they have blue and white feathers.

Smaller with blue and white feathers

Little penguin   Adelie penguin   Emperor penguin

Monkey Mia
is within Shark Bay but it is not named after a monkey. Mia is an Indigenous word meaning home, and Monkey was the name of the boat used to dive for pearls in that area.

Monkey Mia is actually famous for the **dolphins** who visit the beach daily.

Camel Rock

near Bermagui on the south coast of New South Wales, is a rock formation that looks like a sitting camel.

Karta Pintingga

is the Indigenous name for Kangaroo Island, given by the local Kaurna people and means the island of the dead.

It is Australia's third largest island after Tasmania and Melville Island.

Matthew Flinders named the island after the many kangaroos seen and hunted when he and his crew visited in 1802.

Geographic Joys

The Great Barrier Reef

The Great Barrier Reef is the world's largest coral reef system with over 900 islands, 2,900 individual reefs and a total area of 348,000 square kilometres.

It is the ecosystem with the richest biodiversity in the world with over 400 species of corals, 1,500 species of fish and 4,000 types of molluscs.

It became a UNESCO World Heritage Site in 1981. The Great Barrier Reef is bigger than Victoria and Tasmania.

It is actually bigger than the Netherlands, Switzerland and the United Kingdom combined.

World's Longest Continental Volcano Track

Did you know that Australia's continental volcano track is discovered to be the world's longest? It is three times longer than the Yellowstone volcano track in the US.

The Australian chain stretches 2,000 kilometres from Melbourne to the Whitsundays in northern Queensland.

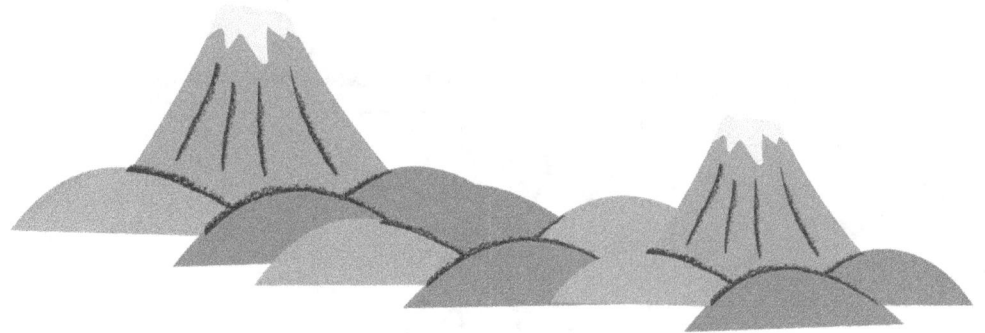

Continental volcanoes are found far from the meeting of the tectonic plates where most volcanoes occur.

Australia's volcano track was formed 33 million years ago by mantle plumes which are upwellings of hot rocks from the earth's core-mantle (3,000 kilometres below the surface). But do not worry, all this happened a long time ago.

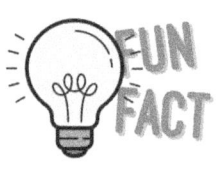 Amongst all the continents in the world, Australia is the only one without any active volcanoes.

Is Uluru the world's largest rock?

The answer is YES.

Uluru is the largest single chunk of rock in Australia and indeed the largest monolith in the world (or more strictly, inselberg, meaning island mountain). .

Mount Augustus in Western Australia is often said to be the world's largest monolith but this is incorrect: it is in fact the world's largest monocline which is a fold in rock strata.

Uluru is 348 metres tall, higher than the Eiffel Tower which is 324 metres tall, the Great Pyramids at 139 metres tall, and the Statue of Liberty at 93 metres tall.

 ### Does It Snow In Australia?
The answer is YES.

The Australian Alps is the only area on the Australian mainland that receives deep snow every year. -23°C is the lowest temperature ever recorded in Australia, at the ski resort Charlottes pass in the Snowy Mountains on 29th June 1994.

Australia's Pink Lakes

If you or your sister likes pink, then go ahead and ask your parents to let you visit one of the pink lakes found in Australia.

Lake Hillier on Middle Island off the coast of Western Australia is the best-known pink lake but is very remote and only accessible by air or by sea using tour operators.

The bubble gum pink colour of the lake is caused by a mix of colourful but harmless bacteria and algae. It is safe to swim in Lake Hillier but drinking the water is not recommended.

Oodnadatta is the hottest place in Australia

Oodnadatta in South Australia holds the record for the highest recorded temperature in Australia at 50.7 °C (123.3 °F).

However the record was matched by Onslow in Western Australia on 13 January, 2022. Third hottest are Mardie and Roebourne in Western Australia's Pilbara, at 50.5°C recorded on 13 January, 2022.

You're right to think that 13 January, 2022 was the hottest day ever recorded in Australia ... unless that record has been broken by the time you read this!

Highest Point in Australia

The peak of Mount Kosciuszko is the highest point in Australia at 2,228 metres (7,310 feet) above sea level. Kosciuszko's mean monthly temperature is often below freezing for eight months of the year.

Note: There are higher mountains in the Australian Antarctic Territory and also on remote Heard Island, but these are not part of the Australian continent.

Australia has more than 10,000 beaches!

There are more than 10,000 beaches along the coastline of Australia which stretches for an amazing 34,000 kilometres (21,000 miles) if you exclude the smaller offshore islands. The most famous beach of them all is Bondi Beach which is just one kilometre long.

Australia has the world's ninth largest road network with 356,000 kilometres of paved road and over 466,000 kilometres of unpaved road.

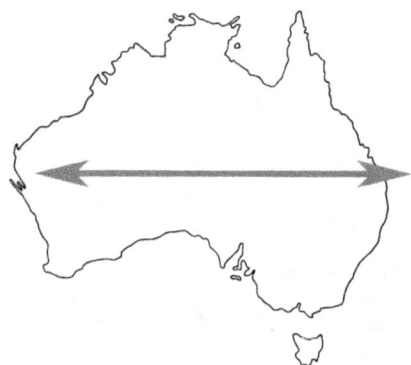

The distance from the most easterly point of Australia to the most westerly is 4,000 kilometres. From the most northerly point to the most southerly point in Tasmania the distance is 3860 kilometres. It's a big country!

Once, Tasmania was part of Australia's mainland. 12,000 years ago, when the ice age ended, ocean levels rose and drowned the landbridge.

Despite being surrounded by water, almost one-fifth of Australia is considered a desert whilst 70% is classified as arid or semi-arid meaning it gets less than 500 millimetres of rain annually.

There are 10 deserts in Australia and the largest is the Great Victorian Desert.

Many deserts in Australia have thunderstorms. However, given the heat, they are often dry storms and the rainfall evaporates before it hits the ground.

The cleanest air on earth is recorded in Tasmania. The air monitoring station at Cape Grim in northwest Tasmania records the cleanest air in all the world, but only when the wind is blowing from the west across the Roaring Forties.

The largest cattle station in Australia is Anna Creek Station in South Australia. At 23,000 square kilometres, it is larger than in Israel.

The population of Australia is around the same size as a single city in China - Shanghai!

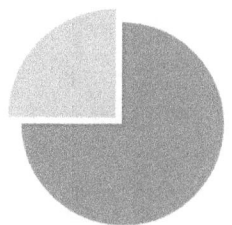

Roughly 25% of Australians were born outside of Australia.

85% of Australians live within 50 kilometres of the coast.

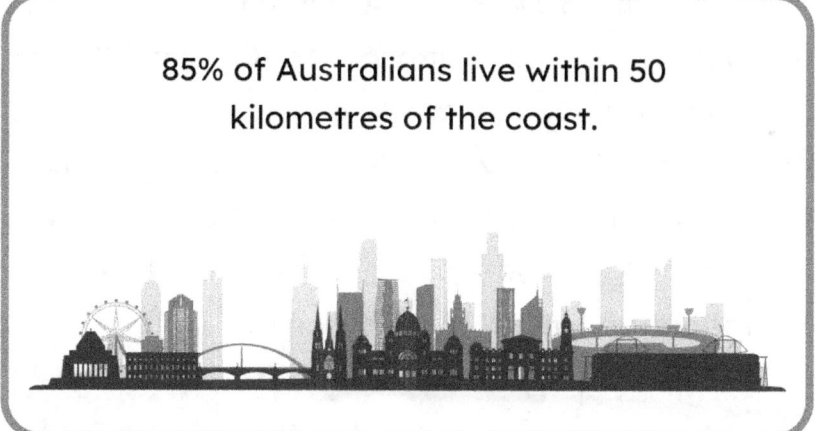

The longest river in Australia is the Murray River which runs for 2,508 kilometres (1,558 miles) through New South Wales, Victoria and South Australia.

New South Wales is the most populated state with 31.8% of Australia's population living there. Victoria is next with 25.8% then Queensland with 20.4% followed by Western Australia with 10.4% and South Australia with 6.9%. Tasmania is the third least populated state with 2.7% followed by the Australian Capital Territory with 1.7%. The Northern Territory has just 1% of the Australian population. These figures are from the 2021 Census of Population.

Incredible Indigenous Australia

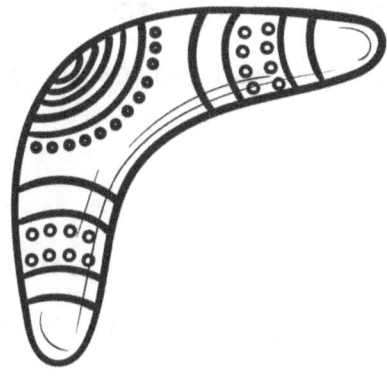

Boomerangs were not invented by Indigenous Australians and have been found in several other areas of the world throughout history. However, the name is from an Indigenous Australian word.

The first recorded writing about boomerangs in Australia was made by Francis Louis Barrallier, a French-born ensign in the New South Wales Corps. When looking for a route over the Blue Mountains, he wrote in his journal on 12 November 1802:
'The natives of this part of the country make use of a weapon which is not employed by and is even unknown to, the natives of Sydney.'

Barrallier continued: 'It is composed of a piece of wood in the form of a half circle which they make as sharp as a sabre on both edges and pointed at each end.'

'They throw it on the ground or in the air, making it revolve on itself, and with such velocity that one cannot see it returning towards the ground; only the whizzing of it is heard.'

'When they throw it along the ground it is exactly like a cannonball, knocking down everything in its passage.'

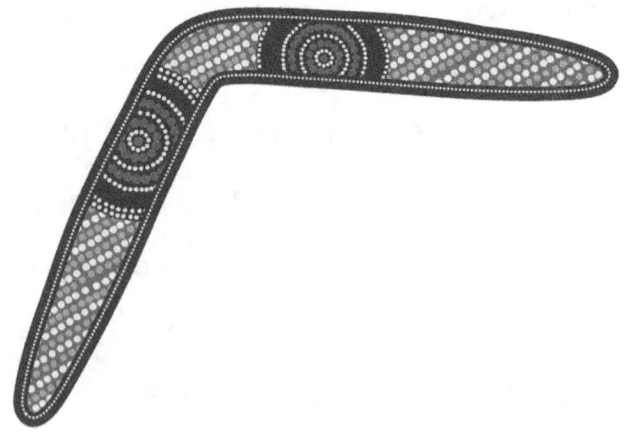

Many of Australia's First Nations peoples played ball games, often using a furry ball made of possum skins. The Wurundjeri people played a game called marngrook that seems to have involved the high kick now seen in Australian Rules football.

> Aboriginal and Torres Strait Islanders make up roughly 3.3% of the Australian population.

> There were 250 distinct Aboriginal language groups throughout Australia when colonists arrived. 150 are still spoken today..

Moomba is the name of an annual festival held in Melbourne. In some Aboriginal languages, it means 'up your bum.'

Many Australian words are derived from Aboriginal languages such as kangaroo, boomerang, yabber, wallaby, kookaburra, and wonga.

Astounding Animals

What percentage of Australian animals are endemic?

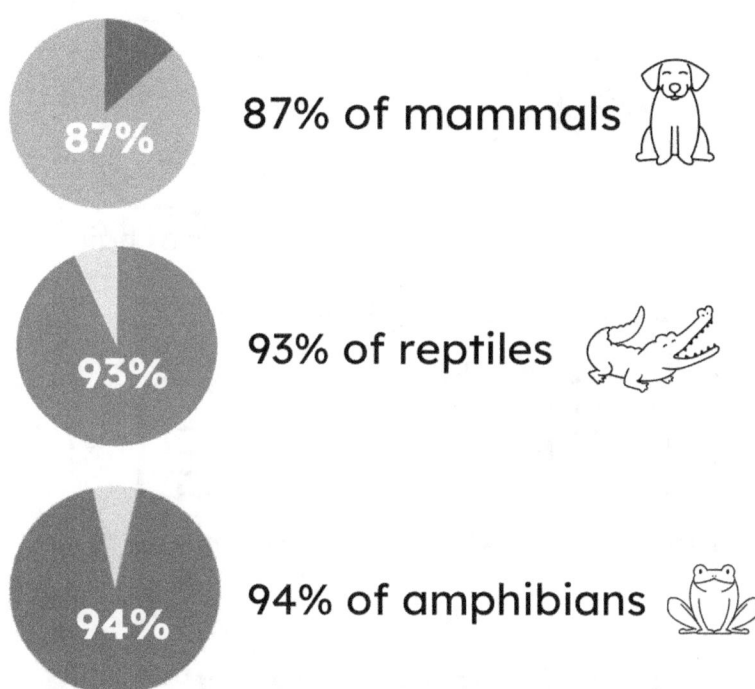

87% — 87% of mammals

93% — 93% of reptiles

94% — 94% of amphibians

What does endemic mean?

Endemic means something that only lives in one particular place. More than 80% of all Australian animals and plants in the world are only found in Australia.

What are mammals?

Mammals are warm-blooded animals, have hair, backbones or spines, and feed their young with milk. Humans are also classified as mammals, as is your pet dog, cat, hamster, & rabbit.

warm-blooded

has fur or hair

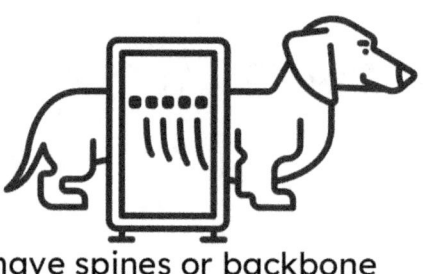
have spines or backbone

feed milk to their young

Whales and dolphins are not classified as fish, they are both mammals.

What are reptiles?

Reptiles are cold-blooded animals that have dry scaly skin and typically lay eggs on land. This includes snakes, lizards, crocodiles, and turtles.

What are amphibians?

Amphibians are cold-blooded animals that hatch from eggs, and then live and breathe in the water during the first part of their lives.

They evolve and live the last part of their lives on land. This includes frogs, toads, newts, and salamanders.

If you are looking for a new pet....

If you think that flies are the biggest pests in Australia, you are wrong.

Dromedary camels (one-humped camels) are even bigger pests, but only in the outback desert areas. Camels were brought over in the 19th century to work as pack animals in great numbers, with Afghan cameleers looking after them. They pulled huge wagons and were essential to many exploratory expeditions.

Motor vehicles arrived so camels were no longer needed and most were let loose into outback areas where they have thrived. There were estimated to be 800,000 feral camels on the loose before the National Feral Camel Action Plan was put in place in 2010. There are now humane camel-culling programs and some areas put up camel fences. The camel population is now estimated to be around 300,000. New industries include farming camels for milk and meat as well as for the tourism industry. If you are looking for a new pet, just pop into the desert and catch a camel.

The Emu: Amazing Anti-Radiation Feathers + Soothing Oil

Emus are huge flightless birds which have very tiny wings. When running at top speed emus do however flap their wings, using them to help balance and change direction. They also flap their mini-wings to help cool themselves down.

Just like your sunglasses, an emu's feathers can help it absorb the sun's radiation. The dark tips of their feathers absorb the sun's radiation and their shaggy mass of feathers insulates the bird so that little heat reaches the skin. The emu's feathers range in colour from darker brown to paler brown with some having reddish tinges. The skin on their heads and necks is blue and can be seen through the sparse feathers there.

Emus are the second largest bird in the world behind the ostrich, growing up to almost two metres in height. The emu's top sprint speed is 50 km/h (31 mph) which is faster than Usain Bolt but slower than an ostrich.

Emu War

In 1932, an 'Emu War' took place in Western Australia when a deployment of soldiers armed with Lewis Guns tried to reduce a population of 20,000 which was threatening the wheat crop. Despite many emus being killed, the emus won the war and numbers continued to rise.

Emu Meat & Oil

Emus are farmed commercially in Australia with their low-fat meat being considered to be very healthy. Emu oil is also made from the bird's fatty tissues.

Indigenous Australians used emu oil to ease inflammation for millennia and now it is sold commercially to ease inflammation and arthritis.

Monotremes

Platypus and echidna are the only mammals in the world that are capable of laying eggs. These two animals are the only members of the monotreme sub-group of mammals.

The Platypus: Cute but Poisonous

Platypus is known to be uniquely charming but highly poisonous.

They inject poison from spurs on their rear legs just above their claws. Platypuses wraps their rear legs around their foe and stabs with these spurs. They can kill small to medium-sized animals and even dogs.

Platypuses do not kill humans but their venom causes swelling, nausea and terrible pain all over the body. So steer clear.

The Box of Death

The box jellyfish found on the Great Barrier Reef is the most dangerous animal in that area. It has a higher kill ratio than saltwater crocodiles, snakes, and big sharks combined.

Beware of the Tasmanian Devil's bite

Tasmanian devils may be small but be careful if you encounter one in the wild as they have the strongest bite force relative to their size of any mammal.

The Tasmanian devil's head and neck are so huge they make up 25% of its body mass. The Tasmanian devil can open its jaws to an angle of 80 degrees and its bite strength is 1200 pounds per square inch. That's the same bite strength as a polar bear and amazingly powerful.

So beware!

Koalas Are Like A Real-life Snorlax

Koalas sleep for about 20 hours per day, just like the Pokémon Snorlax but in real life. Koalas love to sleep not because they want to but because of their diet.

Koalas only eat eucalyptus leaves, which are low in nutrition and have some toxins and a lot of fibre, that require a lot of energy to digest.

The koala has a low-energy lifestyle to match its low-energy diet sleeping almost all day whilst the bacteria in its digestive tract do all the hard work.

Koalas tend to live amongst several trees called their 'home trees.'

Male koalas rub their chest against the trunks of their home trees to leave their scent so that other koalas know the tree is taken.

Incredible Crocs

Saltwater crocodiles have roughly 68 sharp teeth and can exert two tonnes of pressure from a single bite.

These crocodiles are found around the northern areas of Australia from Broome in Western Australia to Rockhampton in Queensland. There are more than one million saltwater crocodiles in the Northern Territory alone. So look out!

Crocodiles kill at least one person every year in Australia, and often more.

Cool camels
Believe it or not, when Saudi Arabia needs camels, Saudis buy them from Australia.

In many original Tarzan movies, the jungle sounds were recordings of the laughing kookaburra.

Weird wombats

Wombats have the largest brains of all marsupials.

We mentioned previously that wombats have square poo but other than that, they are also great bluffers. When threatened they make loud hissing sounds and kick backwards like a donkey.

In retreat, they dive headfirst into their burrow leaving their bum exposed. Thankfully its thick fur and skin are extremely tough!

Wombats have tiny eyes and poor vision. They make up for it with excellent hearing and smell.

Wombats are notorious for digging alternate exits to their burrows when traps are placed at the entrance. Clever wombats!

The common wombat is nicknamed the 'bulldozer of the bush.'

Termite Talk

Cathedral termites in the Northern Territory, Western Australia and Queensland build mounds up to eight metres in height, though most of those you will see when travelling in the Northern Territory are around three metres high.

A termite colony can have between a few hundred to a few million termites and the queens can live up to 50 years!

Magnetic termite mounds are only found in the Northern Territory. The mounds are mysteriously aligned north-south to the earth's magnetic field.

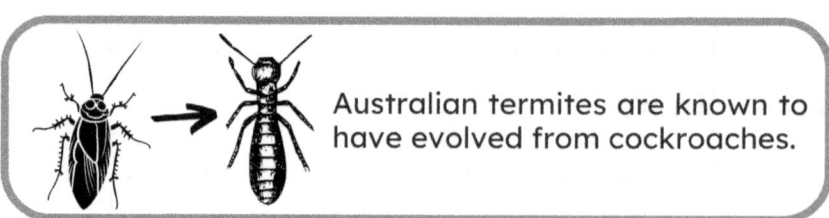

Australian termites are known to have evolved from cockroaches.

Dingoes

Dingoes are not closely related to dogs

Though dingoes look similar to some domesticated dogs they are more closely related to Indian wolves and the rare New Guinea singing dog. Just listen to them and you will hear that they do not bark, they howl.

The dingo is Australia's largest mammalian carnivore and an important apex predator.

Interbreeding with other types of feral dogs means that the dingo gene pool is being diluted and has caused the dingo to be listed on the IUCN Red List of Threatened Species as a vulnerable species.

Dingoes have extremely flexible necks and can turn their heads 180 degrees to look behind them.

Dingos reached Australia from the Indonesian land bridge 12,000 years ago and are the largest carnivore on the continent.

It is believed that 70% of the dingo population in the wild are not pure but rather are dingo-domestic hybrids.

Scary Spiders and Snakes

There are more than 2,000 species of spiders in Australia.

Thankfully only a handful are dangerous!

Australian spiders might look hairy, but these are not real hairs. They are sensory setae that spiders use to collect information about their surrounding environment.

There are more than 140 species of land snake and 32 species of sea snake in Australia but don't worry, of the 100 snakes that are venomous only 12 species can kill humans.

Did you know that snakes flick out their tongues so that they can detect chemicals in the air which helps them to track prey?

Fearsome Fly Facts

Female flies are the ones that drive you crazy. They seek humans in search of proteins that they need to make eggs. The sweat on human bodies is an ideal source.

Australia is home to thousands of species of flies. In the time it takes your brain to swat a fly, it has already seen you coming, reacted, and flown away.

Beaut Birds

The Australian magpie is a skilled mimic and can copy the songs of around 35 other bird species and even some horse and dog noises.

Australia's Animal Emblems

Kangaroos and emus cannot move backwards easily.

Whilst they physically can go backwards if absolutely necessary, they rarely do.

They were used on the coat of arms for exactly that reason, to symbolise constantly moving forward.

By the way, most countries do not eat the animals which feature on their coast of arms, like the American eagle and the lion rampant in Scotland.

But Australians do eat emu and kangaroo.

Crazy Kangaroos

We all know that kangaroos have pretty big feet! They belong to the family Macropodoidea which literally means 'big feet.'

Western grey kangaroos are knowns as 'stinkers.' That's because they have a strong body odour caused by the types of plants they eat.

Joeys or kangaroo babies are only the size of a jellybean when they are born, that's just about 2 centimetres long.

A Giant Leap For.... Kangaroos

Red kangaroos are the largest type of kangaroo although only the males are very large; the females are smaller.

An average male red kangaroo weighs between 55 to 80 kilograms (121 to 198 lb) and is around 1.5 metres tall. The largest red kangaroo ever recorded was 2.1 metres (6.9 feet) tall and weighed 91 kilograms.

Have you ever wondered how far these red kangaroos can leap? Wonder no more. The longest recorded bound made by a red kangaroo was 12.8 metres (42 feet) though bounds of nine metres (30 feet) are more common.

Did You Know?

Echidnas have electroreceptors on the tip of their beak which helps them to locate food underground.

Thorny devil lizards look scary but they are not at all aggressive.

They live in hot, dry areas so their skin is tough and doesn't sweat so they don't lose any of the small amounts of water they drink.

Do Drop Bears Exist?

The answer is NO.

Have you heard about drop bears? You have been conned! Drop bears are mythical creatures reported to be large hairy mammals that drop out of trees and kill people. They must be closely related to the wild Scottish haggis! This urban myth was created to scare and trick American soldiers posted to Australia during World War II and the Vietnam War.

Australia is a biodiversity hotspot with 200,000 species of plants, fungi, animals, fish, insects and other organisms already named.

But taxonomists believe that they have only discovered 30% of the species in Australia so far. So there is plenty of work for scientists to get on with!

Wacky History + Politics Facts

Only in Australia would you find a politician referencing the iconic Iced Vovo biscuit in an election victory speech.

Prime Minister Kevin Rudd mentioned this beloved Australian biscuit in his speech on the night of 24 November, 2007. Iced Vovo sales spiked!

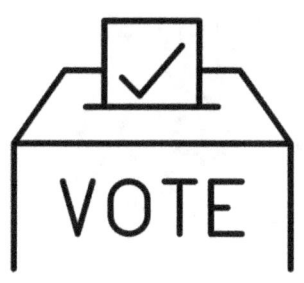

Australia was the second country in the world to give women the right to vote in 1902

South Australian women had been able to vote in state elections since 1894.

Around 80% of the 162,000 convicts shipped to Australia between 1788 and 1868 were thieves.

On the First Fleet John, Russel had stolen one copper saucepan and a checked apron, Robert Scattergood had stolen two live geese and Margaret Darnell had stolen one dozen dessert knives and forks.

The first ever Australian police force was a group of 12 of the most well-behaved convicts known as The Night Watch and then as the Sydney Foot Police.

Calling people 'mate' was banned.

Did you know that back in 2005, the security guards of Canberra's Parliament House were not permitted to call people 'mate'. However, this ban only lasted for a day, for obvious reasons. That's funny. Right, mate?

The bearded bushranger, Ned Kelly, has had more biographies written about him than any other Australian.

Phenomenal Places

Lark Quarry in the outback of Australia has the only fossilised remains of a dinosaur stampede in the world.

There are hundreds of dinosaur footprints fossilised in the rock and they are around 95 million years old.

The Dinosaur Stampede National Museum at Lark Quarry Conservation Park is in outback Queensland.

Ningaloo Reef in Western Australia gets its name from the Aboriginal Wajarri language word meaning deep water or high land jutting into the sea.

Ningaloo Reef is home to whale sharks, pelagic fish like tuna and billfish, humpback whales, dolphins, manta rays, dugong, and turtles, such as the green, the loggerhead and the hawksbill.

The Great Southern Reef

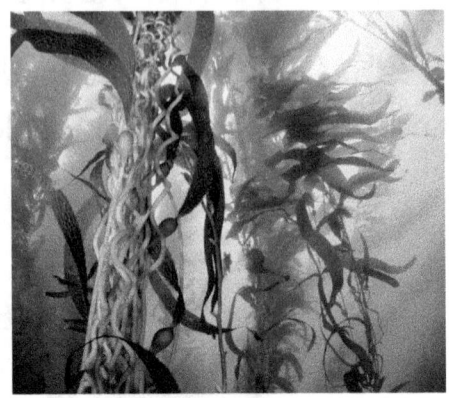

The Great Southern Reef is a series of golden kelp forest reefs that extend around 8,000 km of Australia's southern coastline, covering a total area of 71,000 square kilometres.

70% of Australians live close to an interconnected network of reefs that make up the Great Southern Reef yet a lot of them do not know very much about it.

The world's longest stretch of completely straight railway is found on the Nullabor Plain and runs for 480 kilometres.

The Nullabor Plain is the world's largest single piece of limestone bedrock, a staggering 200,000 square kilometres.

At its widest point, it runs for it is 1,100 km (684 miles). The name comes from the Latin 'nullus arbor', meaning 'no trees.'

The Pinnacles Desert within Nambung National Park in Western Australia has hundreds of limestone pillars rising from the desert sand. Many look like gravestones and the tallest are 3.5 metres high.

The Gold Coast's canal system is so large - it's bigger than Venice & Amsterdam combined.

Fraser Island, also known by its Aboriginal name K'gari, lies off the Queensland coast and is the largest sand island in the world.

Lake Eyre in the southern outback is the lowest point in Australia and is 15m below sea level.

Mount Disappointment in Victoria is so named because the British colonial explorers who first climbed it, Hume and Hovell, believed the view was seriously disappointing. But don't take their word for it.

Lady Elliot Island in the Great Barrier Reef is kept together by three things – dead coral, tree roots, and guano. You guessed it – guano is bird poo!

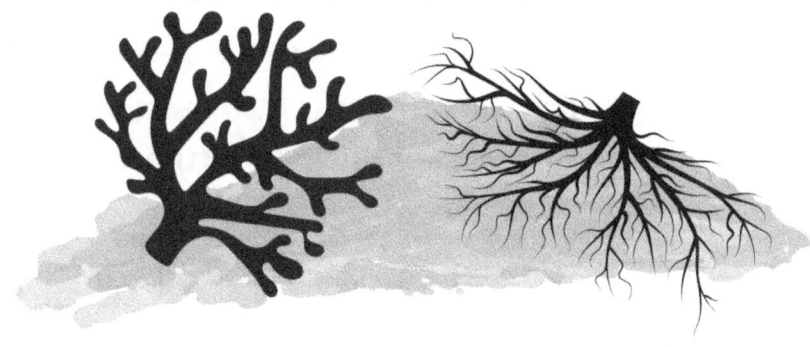

The Blue Mountains get their name from the blue haze you can see around them from the plains below.

This blue haze is caused by oily droplets evaporating from eucalyptus leaves and mixing with water vapour and dust. These scatter short-wavelength light rays which are mainly blue in colour.

Kati Thanda-Lake Eyre in the Flinders Ranges of South Australia is Australia's biggest salt lake measuring 144 kilometres by 77 kilometres and covering 9,500 square kilometres.

When rain fills the lake it becomes home to thousands of birds and fish. But it is spectacular to visit at any time of year.

The Great Ocean Road is the largest war memorial in the world.

This 243-kilometre road was built between 1919 and 1932 by soldiers who had survived the First World War and returned home.

The Memorial Arch at Eastern View marks the start of the Great Ocean Road and commemorates the returned servicemen who laboured to build it.

Strange Sweet Stuff

The humble Anzac biscuit is beloved by Australians and their origins have been written about in a book called Anzac Biscuits: The Power and Spirit of an Everyday National Icon written by historian Allison Reynolds.

Hardtack biscuits were made of oats, flour and syrup and were used by Australian soldiers for many years as a basic ration. Tins of these were sent to Australian soldiers at Gallipolli and afterwards were known as Anzac biscuits.

Have you ever wondered who invented Australia's famous Aeroplane Jelly? It was Sydney tram driver Bert Appleroth who began making jelly crystals in his bathtub in 1927!

The oldest Australian chocolate bar is the Cherry Ripe which was first created in 1924 by the Australian confectioner MacRobertson's and later sold to Cadburys.

There is much debate between New Zealand and Australia about who created the meringue dessert called the pavlova. Both countries claim it was named after Russian ballerina Anna Pavlova.

Did you know that the name of the Caramello Koala is George?

When Freddo Frogs were invented, at the MacRobertson's chocolate factory in Fitzroy, Melbourne in 1930, Australians went so crazy over them that people were jailed for stealing Freddo Frogs.

The original Freddos were shaped more like real frogs than the cartoon-like character we know today.

The creators of Freddo Frogs initially considered creating chocolate mice instead of frogs!

Violet Crumbles was given that name as the inventor's wife adored violet flowers.

Australia sells 670 million individual Tim Tams per year. An iconic Aussie treat, approximately 45 million packs are sold each year. That means each Australian eats about 26 Tim Tams each year!

One of Australia's favourite sweet treats is the lamington, a square of sponge cake rolled in chocolate and then in coconut. Delicious!

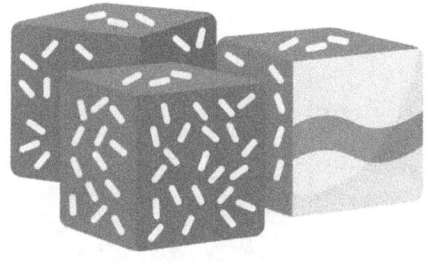

There is much discussion of the origins of the lamington, in fact a book has been written about this, called The Lamington Enigma: a survey of the evidence by Professor Maurice French. There is agreement that the cake was named after Lord Lamington, the Governor of Queensland from 1896 to 1901, or perhaps after his wife Lady Lamington. Perhaps it was the Lady who named them as Lord Lamington is reputed to have described this treat as 'bloody, poofy woolly biscuits'. Woolly they are, but a biscuit, never!

Freaky Farming + Food Facts

60% of food produced in Australia is exported and feeds a massive 40 million people around the world each day.

On average, each Australian farmers produce enough food each year to feed 600 people for that whole year.

Australia is the fourth largest exporter of wine globally, totalling 760 million litres shipped overseas each year.

What is the food that all Australians adore but everyone in the rest of the world does not? It's Vegemite!

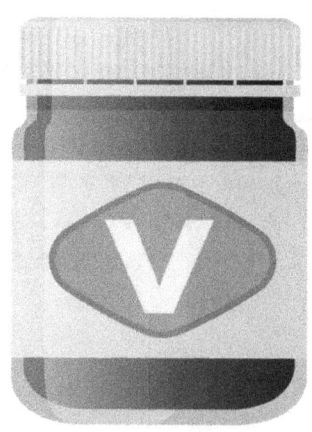

Vegemite was created in 1923 in Melbourne using the leftover yeast from making beer. By 1928, Vegemite was not selling well so it was renamed Parwill. The aim was to outsell Marmite with a slogan of 'Ma might, but Parwill.' It didn't work. And so, in 1935, they went back to Vegemite.

Australia's delicious Chiko roll was invented by Frank McEnroe in 1951. He originally called it the Chicken Roll even though there was no chicken in it.

The shape was based on the Chinese spring roll, and the filling is vegetarian.

Australians must love fish fingers as the amount sold in Australia each year could cover Tasmania.

Do you know what Australians put on their hamburgers that other countries don't? Beetroot!

Granny Smith apples originated in Sydney in 1868 in the orchard of Maria Smith in Ryde. She saw the genetic mutation of a crab apple grow as a seedling and cultivated it.

Crazy Culture

Ugg boots, made from sheepskin, originated in Australia and became popular in the 1960s when surf champions wore them to keep their feet warm when waiting on the beach.

Ugg is a generic name for sheepskin boots and is not trademarked in Australia but UGG is trademarked in 100 other countries by the American company Deckers Brand.

 Before finding fame as an actor, Paul Hogan from Crocodile Dundee worked as a painter on the Sydney Harbour Bridge.

Do you know the meaning behind the words of the song title 'Waltzing Matilda'? Waltzing is slang for travelling on foot and matilda is slang for swag, meaning a rolled blanket that swagmen carried and slept in.

There is no official language in Australia although English is spoken as a first language in 80% of homes and is used as the primary language of the government. The 2021 Census showed that over 400 languages are spoken in Australian of which over 160 are indigenous languages.

Was the first person who documented the use of the word "selfie" Australian?

The answer is YES.

Do you love taking selfies? Some people say that selfies were invented by Robert Cornelius, an American photography enthusiast who took his self-portrait in 1839.

But the first documented use of the word selfie was by Australian man Nathan Hope in 2002. He had an accident while celebrating his mate's twenty-first birthday and then he posted a photograph of himself showing his stitched-up lip. His actual wording, on a 2002 ABC online forum was, 'Sorry about the focus, it was a selfie.' Whilst Nathan did not invent the word (it was in common use at the time), his use of it was the first written example.

Tough Trees

The mountain ash (Eucalyptus regnans) found in Tasmania and Victoria is the tallest hardwood tree in Australia and the tallest flowering plant in the world. It can reach heights of up to 114 metres tall (375 feet).

There is a Napoleon Pear tree in a garden in Hobart which is more than 120 years old and continues to produce 1.5 tonnes of fruit annually.

Tasmania is home to one of the oldest plants in the world, Kings holly (Lomatia tasmanica), believed to be at least 43,000 years old.

In the wet tropics of the Queensland rainforests, you can find the highest concentration of primitive flowering plant families in the world.

The Australia eucalypt or gum tree has over 500 species. Gum trees produce some of the toughest hardwood in the world.

The second tallest tree in the world, the Huon pine, grows in the rainforests of southwest Tasmania.

Sydney Opera House Oddities

Sydney Opera House was inspired by nature and is covered in one million tiles. Jørn Utzon beat more than 200 other architects to win an international competition for the design of the Sydney Opera House in 1957. The magnificent curves of the roof of the Opera House are known as the sails, but the architect said he was inspired by birds, clouds, walnuts and trees.

To explain his ideas he bent a plastic ruler over the edge of a table to show its curve. These sails remind people of seashells and ships' sails and they blend in seamlessly with their harbour surrounds.

The original estimate to build the Sydney Opera House was $7 million. The final cost was $102 million.

Where Sydney Opera House stands is called Bennelong Point after the Aboriginal man Woollarawarre Bennelong who was kidnapped by Governor Phillip when colonists first arrived in 1788. The original Indigenous name was Tubowgule though early colonists named it Limeburners Point.

The sails of the opera house are around 1.62 hectares in size and are covered by more than 1,056,000 white tiles. These tiles are checked by hand by a team of engineers.

Sydney Opera House officially opened in 1973 and holds 1,500 shows per year for close to 11 million visitors. There is also a regular aquatic visitor, a New Zealand fur seal who often basks in the sun on the northern steps. He has been nicknamed 'Benny' after Bennelong Point and is yet to attend any operas, concerts or comedy shows.

Sydney Opera House is a UNESCO World Heritage site and is Australia's most iconic building.

Stunning Cities

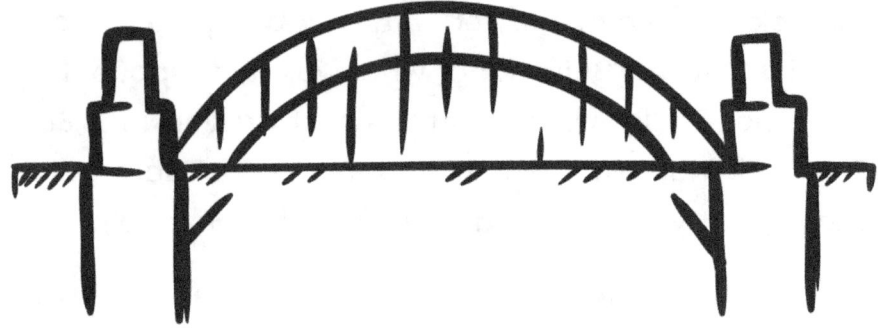

Did you know that locals call the Sydney Harbour Bridge 'The Coathanger?'

It took 272,000 litres of paint to paint the bridge before it was opened on 19 March, 1932. Nowadays it takes 30,000 litres of paint to touch up and repaint.

Sydney Harbour Bridge took 1,400 labourers to build over eight years.

The four huge granite-faced pylons at each end of Sydney Harbour Bridge don't support the bridge. They are there for aesthetic reasons only.

Swimming is very popular at Sydney's ocean and harbour beaches, but things did not start that way.

Between 1838 and 1902 it was forbidden to swim between 6am and 8pm which is a shame as sharks feed at dawn and dusk so the hours during the day are the safest for swimming.

Melbourne has the largest Greek-speaking population of any city outside Greece and Cyprus.

 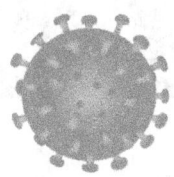

Did you know that Melbourne endured six separate coronavirus lockdowns, totalling 262 days, between March 2020 and October 2021? That is a world record that Melbournians would have preferred not winning.

Canberra became Australia's capital to resolve disputes between Sydney and Melbourne which both wanted to be the country's administrative centre.

Telstra Tower

Perth in Western Australia is one of the most isolated cities in the world.

The closest Australian city is Adelaide which is 2,200 kilometres away.

Final Five Fun Facts

❶ Australia invented the world's first waterproof polymer bank notes in 1988. They are both long-lasting and hygienic as they are resistant to dirt and moisture.

❷ Australians invented notepads, dual-flushing toilets, the pacemaker, the cochlear implant, spray-on skin for burns patients, black box flight recorders, baby safety car capsules and the Hills hoist rotary clothes hoist.

❸ 'The Lucky Country' is the best-known nickname for Australia. But there are others too, like 'The Oldest Continent,' 'The Lost Lands,' 'The Last Frontier,' 'Oz,' and 'Down Under.'

4. The annual Australian Day Cockroach Races held at the Story Bridge Hotel in Brisbane are a popular event, featuring a steeplechase and a sprint for the cockroach participants.

5. Did you know there is a Boomerang Association of Australia? Other countries have boomerang associations too and a World Boomerang Championship is held in a different country every two years.

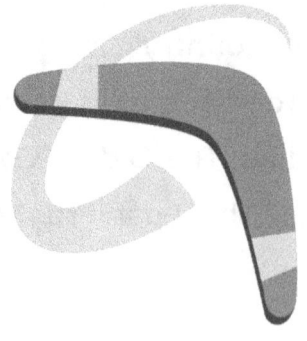

Thank you!

I hope that you have enjoyed reading this book.

Please do leave a review on Amazon if you can, it really helps!

Find out much more about places to visit with kids both in Sydney and throughout Australia on **Hello Sydney Kids.**

ABOUT THE AUTHOR

Seana Smith

Seana Smith was born and brought up in Scotland and now lives in New South Wales, Australia.

She studied Classics and Old and Medieval English at the University of Oxford and then worked as a researcher and producer at Channel 9 and the BBC.

None of this prepared her for motherhood at all but she did her best with her four children who are now young adults and teenagers.

Seana runs the popular website Hello Sydney Kids and the more niche Swim the World and Sober Journeys.

She is also the author of the Australian Autism Handbook, Sydney for Under Fives and Beyond the Baby Blues, all published by Ventura Press.

Disclaimer

All information in this book is intended for entertainment purposes only. Facts stated here are not meant to offend individuals, businesses, companies, organizations, and groups.

All reasonable efforts have been exerted to ensure that the content of this book at the time of publishing are all true and verified.

However, due to the nature of the topic, some facts may not be updated, especially when it comes to World Records as we are all constantly improving and taking on bigger challenges in life.

If there are facts here that you wish to correct kindly use the contact form found on my website at www.hellosydneykids.com.au.

Thank you and I hope you and your kids enjoy reading the facts here as much as we all did.

www.ingramcontent.com/pod-product-compliance
Lightning Source LLC
Chambersburg PA
CBHW070310010526
44107CB00056B/2550